Ackno

Tyrone, my son.

Who came into my life at a time that I had almost given up on it. His presence gave me an entire new meaning and focus to life at a time that I struggled to find either. Yet more than this, he also became and continues to be the catalyst and raison d'etre for my work beyond anything I could have imagined. Thank you, Tyrone.

Lynda, my mother.

My Mother has played a big part in my writing. She is one of the most well-read people I know and has a great passion for poetry. Her continuous approval of my writings are beyond inspiring. She always stood by me throughout the choices I had made in life (however dark they were). I thank her for not only being my Mother, but being my Matriarch and my best friend.

Ian, my father.

My Father is my friend and a huge influence regarding the spiritual input regarding my writing. The direction he has given relating to the bigger picture is reflected in each written expression. He is a teacher, a friend and my Father.

Grandpa John Gribbon.

My wonderful Grandpa who was a true lover of literature and a connoisseur in matters of poetry. Each time I find myself picking up a pen and paper I practically see his wise, subtle and very warm smile looking down at me. Thank you Grandpa. I practically feel you within each word expressed.

Grandfather David Brown.

My beautiful Grandfather David who encouraged love for all living sentient beings. He was an animal lover and a very effective and successful activist. He was also a great lover of poetry particularly Robert Burns. Love shone through him, his heart and his mind. Each time I feel sadness at his absence I simply read his favourite Robert Burns poem 'To a Louse' and smile at him from my heart. Thank you for everything you stand for.

INSIDEOUT

INSIDE OUT

POEMS

GEORGIA BROWN

Matador
Unit E2 Airfield Business Park,
Harrison Road, Market Harborough,
Leicestershire. LE16 7UL
Tel: 0116 2792299
Email: books@troubador.co.uk
Web: www.troubador.co.uk/matador
Twitter: @matadorbooks

ISBN 9781803130521

British Library Cataloguing in Publication Data.
A catalogue record for this book is available from the British Library.

Printed and bound in Great Britain by 4edge Limited
Typeset in 12pt Adobe Caslon Pro by Troubador Publishing Ltd, Leicester, UK

Matador is an imprint of Troubador Publishing Ltd

This book is dedicated to my family

Preface

This book of poems is a creation of unusual beauty and at the same time a story of a profound inner change. It is a moving picture of the culmination of an artistic and spiritual transformation from that of a wild, young, unfocused rebel into a highly talented, skilful and insightful poet. A poet who has lived and experienced life in ways and circumstances that only a few of us would imagine possible. With determination and courage she has met and dealt with a whole host of challenges and privations, finally coming, it would seem, to a deep understanding of life in all of its mysterious ways.

As the daughter of my oldest friend I have known the author from when she was a small child to her present day incarnation as the Writer of Inside Out and during that time she has been a school truant, a teenage rebel, a ferocious, albeit short lived student of the electric guitar, a runaway, a homeless wanderer through the London streets, a squatter, a gymnast, a personal fitness coach, the manager of a thrift shop, a marathon runner, a weight lifter, a cat fighter, a fashion model, a martial arts expert, a loving mother of a fine young man, a skilful Kung Fu practitioner and now a poet indeed a live poet bringing her works to dramatic interpretation on stage as well as on paper. With regard to this last manifestation of her creative being it is, for a fellow writer and former magazine editor such as myself, a most impressive achievement as she left school barely literate due to her frequent and lengthy absences from the halls of learning. Yet now her command of vocabulary is such that she is capable of expressing the most delicate shades of human emotions in her wide-ranging poems.

Of course, it cannot be said that this collection is without flaws. There are occasional rhymes that don't quite work as they should. Sometimes a rhythm is a little off and sometimes the meaning and intention of a poems isn't quite clear. But all of that should only be considered within the perspective of an otherwise highly successful whole. Its missteps notwithstanding this is nonetheless an intriguing, powerfully vivid account of a quest for meaning, for a justification of existence mixed in with the simple need of one young woman to love and be loved for her self alone, In short, to find a place of sanity and some kind of revelatory wisdom in this increasingly crazy world.

Indeed Inside Out is a Heroines Journey - in the great tradition of the time honoured spiritual quest as set out by Joseph Campbell in The Hero with a Thousand Faces.

A struggle from darkness into light.
From deep earth to the blue sky.
And as Thich Nat Hanh said
about growth and creativity:
No Mud. No Lotus

William Corner Clarke,
writer and poet.
January 2023
Virginia, U.S.A

A STRANGER ON THE BRIDGE

It happened not too long ago
When I'd become my pain

I watched a landscape filled with snow
As all my hope was drained

I felt the sadness of the earth
Combined with that in me

I asked the gods to give re-birth
Or just to set me free

A moment everyone has known
Yet never spoken loud

The part of self we've never shown
Too frightened or too proud

Reflecting on the times gone by
While pondering on my life

Without delay, my heart then cried
While shackled by my strife

The time had come, or so I thought,
Upon that bridge alone

I stared to yearning skies and sought
For skies to take me home

Then in one final lost attempt
I whispered with defeat

'Please help me, if this life is meant'
For I am truly beat

I then proceeded, not a care,
Restraint was far from curbed

Yet stopped, I felt someone was there
My ending now disturbed

A shadow only feet away
The sound of someone's tear

I focused, and without delay
On sadness standing near

I took a risk, though still unknown
I knew not who was there

I found a boy, and so alone
With heartache in his stare

I asked the gods to lend their eyes
While speaking words of ease

I asked 'Please now destroy the ties
That brought him to his knees'

I sat beside him whilst he talked
Of all his words unheard

We sat, we paused, we paced, then walked
Until his pain was blurred

I watched him go from grey to blue
His seasons changed inside

'Did you help me, or I help you'
He asked while smiling wide

I realised, I'd filled a cause
My prayers that night were met

The grief in me was put on pause
The scene was truly set

By reaching out, I'd reached inside
His cries helped me to weep

By hearing him I heard the tide
Of tears I'd buried deep

ANGEL IN THE DUST

He stood there alone whilst dark angels would fly
Though the volume was flat, his whole tone remained high

The words of the takers were soon to withdraw
In their leaving him nothing they gave him much more

His truth and his outlook was far from naïve
He embraced love through giving while they gave to receive

It was then his eyes opened to society's deal
True hearts remain hidden and the rest seemed unreal

Yet beneath the conditions they can all beat as one
That connection flows freely when the riches have gone

Compassion comes easy for those living bliss
Yet such actions are few for the lost and dismissed

The angel in dust holds the hands of the wrong
On a street left unnoticed giving hope in his song

The angel unkempt who has dirt on his face
Turns his threads and his tatters into satin and lace

The angel with a halo not shining so bright
Still flew from the heavens of god-given light

While he's not educated, well groomed, or from class
He rejects such illusions to give love to the mass

He only knows value in the joy that peace brings
While transforming the crooks and the villains to kings

Invisible angel unseen in your flight
Using arrows of love used to counter the fight

Recognition means nothing when your reason is clear
When the pain becomes distant, your angel is near

BANGING HEART

The man and mountain blend as one
A saving grace undying
A force so huge is never gone
A flame without the trying

Though I myself had known your light
Our meetings were not plenty
Yet now your soul has taken flight
A space on earth stands empty

I often heard the stories told
Of lives you helped repairing
A dusty diamond wrapped in gold
So grounded yet so daring

A Judo teaching giant spark
A Northern light respected
Yet those you knew who felt the dark
Were never once neglected

A banging heart who banged down walls
To counter limitation
A banging mind banged opened doors
To reach his destinations

A banging smile smashed through the grief
Of those who banged destruction
Your banging light raised self-belief
While smashing through corruption

A stable castle standing tall
To youths who came to know you
They learned to strike they learned to fall
Some even learned to throw you

A party man and perfect host
With guests of varied statue
Revered, yet never one to boast,
In truth you didn't have to

For me, I'm one of hundreds more,
You touched in darker seasons
A kid disrupted to her core
No structure, point or reason

When introduced upon that day
I felt ashamed and broken
Yet all the demons ran away
In banging words you'd spoken

My heart now beats for those so dear
The ones who can't believe this
For loved ones in a mist unclear
Who cannot yet perceive this

To fellow Judo fighting dons
You grappled with and defeated
To each musician sharing songs
At every party greeted

To paragliding human birds
Who flew up there beside you
To those who hung upon your word
To those who lived inside you

To those who smile as they recall
Some sturdy words you gave them
To those you cushioned in their fall
Whilst unaware you saved them

Your banging force can't fade away
Such strength cannot be fleeting
Your light remained upon the day
Your mighty heart stopped beating

BEGIN TO LET IT GO

Begin to let it go for now
Although you don't yet know

Begin the process, then allow
The sufferance to go

Just ask the gods to lead the way
While giving some idea

Then take each challenge day by day
Until your path is clear

Just make the choice, to understand
The things you can't yet see

Then open up to reaching hands
They've come to set you free

The liberation doesn't start
With knowledge in your mind

It comes to life within the heart
It's there your hands are bind

The patterns you repeat can cease
Just choose to reach inside

Then swim in joy once you release
The sadness that you hide

I know it isn't cut and dried
Yet change begins with choice

It's there we face all we've denied
Within a small child's voice

BEING YOU

Being you, you will surpass
Those seeing you in darker mass
While bending corners cold and sharp
To mend the fallen broken hearts

Being you, there will be times
The key in you is found in crimes
The blackened sky brings forth the stars
In lack you'll find the light you are

Being you, we'll hear your shouts
Where glee holds hands with all your doubts
The flaws in this will see you rise
While soaring through the Eagle's skies

Being you, I'm sure you see
Just seeing you brings life to me
Your resurrection from decline
Makes being you help me find mine

BLESSED BE YOU ANGELS

Blessed be, to all the angels
who now fly for you and me
While stepping into darker times
so they can set us free

The angels who have all the sky
yet enter lifeless ground
For fallen angels they will fly,
the lost can now be found

Blessed be, to all the angels who
can light the skies in force
Who comfort every crying soul
left tarnished with remorse

Who lift the shadows and the shame
from those who stand condemned
Who trade redemption for the
blame in selfless acts they send

Blessed be, to all the angels who
form sunshine through the rain
While casting beauty through the
storms to help us grow through pain

For they may come in strange
attire and speak in different tongues
Yet they have wings to lift us
higher and love within their songs

Blessed be, to every angel
be they nameless, rogues, or saints
Whose love shines through the judgements
made by what the world dictates

The rebels and the ones who
hide and those now standing tall
Be blessed, for truth deep down inside,
all heartbeats have their call

Blessed be to those left drifting,
feeling faceless in a crowd
The angels watch you closely,
in their silence they are proud

Blessed be to you who feel alone,
you're never set apart
The void inside makes space for
angels living in your heart

CALLING OF ANGELS

I call upon the light that be
The ones who have the love to see
To now denounce each cold attack
Thrown out to those who won't fight back

With strong conviction I shall ask
For help, so they can face this task
Although I fall down on my knees
In skies, I ask they gain appease

Ye guardian angels, I now insist
You shield them all from angry fists
From strikes that come from hidden hands
Protect the souls of falling lands

Dear guardian angels, please forgive
For how some humans choose to live
Instead please resurrect these hearts
Until each toxic thought departs

Dear guardian angels, share your eyes
So they may see beyond the lies
Please, gently use your healing voice
Remind them that they still have choice

Dear guides, demand the wrong repent
For every painful cruel intent
Yet dissolution need not be
Where absolution sets them free

Dear guardian angels, teach us now
To love each neighbour, show us how
Including those who stand depraved
For every soul must now be saved

Dear guides, please lift us from this maze
Designed to disconnect and daze
Please, end destructive thoughts engrained
Dear angels, leave this world unchained

CHILD'S EYES

Sorrow falls into your eyes
This so unseen for years
No more alone sweet little child
I'll take from you those tears

A presence falls around your frame
Of grace, of gentle tones
So easy then to overlook
The place your sadness roams

A smile so warm takes centre stage
Yet heartache by your side
The ghost of what was long ago
Is present yet denied

Sweet little girl please turn around
I'll give to you these hands
I hear your each and every word
Once lost in life's demands

Angelic child, unseen and grown
The monsters soon will fade
Come forth and open dusty doors
While walking from the shade

My graceful friend with child's eyes
You shared your gift with me
I'll cherish that, protect it close
Until your monsters flee

COALITION OF LOVE

So do you feel it in the air
The love some leaders cease to share
The condemnation of accord
To those left helpless, those left flawed

While I for one believe in all
Each living heartbeat has its call
Yet separation reigns the lands
Corruption ties the angels hands

The families' loved ones face a storm
Yet enmity becomes the norm
I don't deny some things are real
Yet where's the love for what they feel

What happens when the joyful times
Become a memory in our minds
While locking down the space for new
Then binding down the wings in you

A virus came and yes it's fact
Yet also used to now distract
From what they know the truth to be
Within the hearts of you and me

No one can win, not in the end
They can't control what earth will send
In storms she shouts of all her pain
Straight from the mouths of hurricanes

A coalition could exist
If blindness failed to still persist
In grabbing diamonds made of dust
While basing life on gold and lust

A coalition, shaking hands
A fellowship that saves our lands
To be as one, a dharma-state
With LOVE before it's way too late

DESTINATION – YOU

The actions and the titles
Are just lands you travelled through
It often takes such cycles
Before you finally get to you

Some dwellings had foundations
That were rocky to the core
While homes that lacked vibration
Gave you strength to seek much more

Then came the sky-rise giants
Overshadowing those who'd stare
While a prisoner to defiance
At the cries of your despair

Your submission soon became the shift
It threw you into fields
With pretty souls confused adrift
In homes attached to wheels

It wasn't long before you yearned
A hibernation place
You lived in walls where masters learned
To wear their pain with grace

Yet still this craving felt before
Demanded distant soil
The shamans cave with strong allure
Gave hope in your recoil

You found a healer, yet craved messiah
While desperate for his trance
You dressed in Zen, yet bled desire
Within your broken stance

He sat before you wearing beads
His incense filled the room
His jars were full with magic seeds
Designed to end the doom

His movements came in different shades
Like rainbows tied to skin
You noticed all the searching fade
While something cried within

He spoke intensely whilst at one
With all your silenced tears
Then sang the answers in a song
You'd searched for all those years

He showed you in the crystal ball
The many roads you'd stepped
The strength to overcome each fall
Yet every tear wept

He handed you his onyx stone
Your hands began to shake
Then gently said 'You're not alone'
As guides do not forsake

He said with words so light yet deep
'I have no magic spear'
Yet as you wakened from your sleep
The voodoo disappeared

You looked into his piercing gaze
While searching for the lord
Yet mirroring of the self-erase
Self-loathing now left floored

Your hands then slashed the chains so taut
Your presence now anew
The wisdom and the shrine you'd sought
Is destination - you

DIS-EASE

The laughing Buddha, God, or guides
What ever you may be

Help us to swim from poisoned tides
Then teach us to be free

Within redemption, truth or dreams
Help us to now forgive

The angry tongues whose outrage screams
At all the good that lives

Golden heaven, earth and skies
I truly don't belong

In lands that make the angels cry
Each time they sing their song

Yet every word can leave a mark
That stains this untouched skin

So please my guides, shine in the dark
When patience wears so thin

Pagan, Hindu, Dao or Christ
Remind me now of love

In times collective rage is rife
Send feeling from above

For something soaks straight through my flesh
Each time I walk in streets

Of souls so lost in man-made stress
Subject to self-defeats

Corruption, cruelty based on wealth
From those lost in desire

Redemption saves you from yourself
When castles set on fire

Dear golden guides, come in your fleet
While beating poisoned seas

Bring those who fall back to their feet
Take from them this dis-ease

DON'T LET THE VENOM SCORN YOU

You are beautiful
You're suitable
For life's uncovered stage

With a heart so warm
Please, don't be torn
By those who shout in rage

You are shining
For those pining
To find something deep inside

Now you can show them
And you know them
For the beauty that they hide

Yes, you're older
Yet you're bolder
Inner light dictates the flesh

All you're giving
Helps the living
To rise up from what was less

Yet, some are loathing
In sheep's clothing
All the love you scream & shout

Remain untarnished
By those varnished
As a means to stamp you out

They do not see this
Yet to be this
Will reflect each poisoned song

So watch with sorrow
Their tomorrow
Hands them back each darkened wrong

Yet, you won't hate
Nor underrate
Despite the venom that they speak

Your every sentence
Gives repentance
To the angry and the weak

DUSKY LIGHTS & CHOICES

Henceforth I see, right there in mass
The dusky lights are yearning

Colossal wrench and bold as brass
I pause within my turning

The feather falls from endless sky
To rouse my expiration

Yet dusky lights they blind the eye
In moments hope is taken

Small wonder then why I recoil
While clutching divination

When dusky lights exist to spoil
My flashes of elation

Whilst manifesting purgatory
I hear the angels voices

Beyond those dusky lights, I see
The gifts they bring with choices

Henceforth I see they come in mass
The skyline almost breathing

The dusky lights begin to pass
Dismay inside me leaving

The journey turns a different shade
Like paint drops on perception

The roads we walk are those we've made
Choose wisely your projection

FOR HIM, FOR HER & YOU

I was written through this hand
To truly make you now aware
That if your feet hit sinking sand
Someone will always care

I was written right in sync
With something that you stand to face
To say, whatever you may think
You'll reach a better place

I was written on a day
You couldn't see nor feel an end
When heavy clouds won't go away
Embrace this love I send

I was written whilst you cried
Behind a weeping lonely door
To say 'I'll be there by your side
To lift you from the floor'

I was written in the hope
That I could jog your drifting mind
In times you question how you'll cope
As strength inside you'll find

I was written for the one
Who fixes hurting broken bones
You heal their hearts within your song
But don't forget your own

She wrote me for the less desired
All tangled up in rage
It's not too late to be inspired
I'll help you turn that page

I was written from above
For those who feel they're truly through
This pen leaks ink combined with love
For him, for her, and you

FORBIDDEN PRIEST/HOLY MAN

Forbidden sacred holy man
Her prayer is soaked in wrong

Your warm and open holy hand
Gives life to all her songs

Yet dear man of untouched flesh
The point is surely missed

The safety net she could caress
Gains breath within your kiss

Oh, ye who walks on water pure
Baptising many lost

Before you open yearning doors
First contemplate the cost

For she has fallen on the soil
Of temporary sand

One day with strength she will recoil
In light of God's command

Integrity runs through her veins
Beyond the books ideal

She welcomes all the strikes and pain
With faith her God is real

No jinn inside too hard to face
Redemption nothing new

She knows she'll die within disgrace
Then rise again in truth

Yet you dear priest are truly torn
Between the wrong and right

Your hidden need will leave you scorned
You'll fall from such a height

The truth will surely set you free
You know the steps to take

Her virgin flesh is not your glee
But sin, make no mistake

Forbidden sacred holy man
Expose your hidden wrongs

Perceived as warm with open hands
Bring truth to all your songs

Oh godly man of untouched skin
Embrace the light you've known

Denounce the hex, rise from the sin
Of chances you have blown

FORGIVENESS

I never wore a halo
You could never be a saint
In the name of all that matters
You mean more than my complaint

I could never keep my balance
On the pedestal you made
You could never stay so gallant
On red carpets I had laid

I was never really able
To speak sunshine all the time
While occasionally you made mistakes
They weren't the darkest crimes!

Admittedly when windswept
I loose sense of all composure
Understandably when words are sharp
You morph into exposure

Yet how can it hold significance
Within the greater scheme
Shall we battle in the nightmare
Or keep fighting for the dream

The problem is the halo
Sitting heavy on my head
Dictating each angelic word
When truths must now be said

While you have not been knighted
You don't have to be the saint
The value of forgiveness
Is more precious than complaint

FRIEND

Friend is merely just a word
Unspoken proves what's true
Cold days are pain when love is blurred
Kiss first the friend in you

The friendship seen on surface land
Has sweet attractive shades
Enclosed are palms from golden hands
When rainbows start to fade

A friend is not what they may seem
Remember who is loyal
Put first the self within your dream
Embrace your mortal coil

Does every person hear their call
Do we dig deep to see
Enclosed the greatest friend of all
Can truly set you free

Enhanced and programmed words proceed
Perfected games are played
The nursing hands may watch you bleed
If comfort starts to fade

Oblivion runs straight through the veins
No conscious act is fired
Lost hearts support to get the gains
Engrossed by their desires

A friend may come while bearing gifts
Vivacious in their stride
Embrace the friend that never shifts
Embody what's inside

GRATUITOUS KU

This act was gratuitous
Poisoned and ruinous

It's a game that you misunderstood
Where the yin removes fluidness
Ku is unscrupulous

In your strike be prepared for your flood
An impulsive reaction
For self-satisfaction

Poison arrows cascade in the night
Yet the left-hand transaction
Becomes the distraction

While the Ba-Gua reflects back the light
The Right-hand is conscious
In karmic responses

It embodies the spirit of you
While the dark incantation
Carries weak preparation

Where the hand-seal returns all the Wu
So with actions gratuitous
Poisoned and ruinous

Who is it that you truly deceive
Be aware before doing this
Truly know before brewing this
The Jincan you give you receive

A HUMMINGBIRD HAS LOST HER SONG

So faraway from flower beds
Alone where dreams of laughter fled

A ghost that stands alone in life
Outside a smile, inside is strife

No purpose, yet with so much hope
Too far to reach the rescue rope

With so much love she stands alone
Where flowers grew, the weeds have grown

Another day begins once more
She sees the sky, yet hits the floor

Performing on an empty stage
She hears her music start to fade

While reminiscing times now gone
When all her loved ones flowed as one

The light within her has no place
The paint now fades upon her face

She stands observing her surrounds
With many lessons so profound

Yet sees a landscape stark, bereft
No dreams to touch, there's nothing left

How can it be, when after all
She only wished to stop their fall

What feels so right is thrust with wrong
A hummingbird has lost her song

HARMONY

God give us unity
Whoever you may be
Mohammed, Jesus,
Buddha, you may even be Bruce Lee

Give us all a oneness
With eyes so open wide
At a time when this hostility
Puts healing love aside

God, please give us empathy
With warmness in the heart
When these words of cursing leaders
Tear the light within apart

When belief born from our fear
Can attack the needed cord
Show us love for our outsiders
In this crisis now ignored

God, please give us unity
Put ideals to good use
Moses, Krishna, Jesus
While some may call you Zeus

Set aside these judgments
To the ones now fully armed
Whilst you bless them with your insight
Before many more are harmed

Won't you boycott void opinions
Made by those so unaware?
Replace these cold dictators
With the sounds of those who care

God help them see beauty
Be their skin tone black or white
Combine the many colours
Until they blend to make a light

God, please give us something
Before human thread departs
Be you Gandhi, be you Jesus
Beat this strength into our hearts

HOPE

While caves are falling all around
Presumed control now fades
An inner calling can be found
Where truth was once delayed

While made to stop as doors close tight
With silence at our ear
So soon we'll see the pause, the light
Beyond a wave of fear

If clutching at those prison bars
That we believed were safe
Has left us lost to who we are
It's time to touch our faith

If all you owned turns into dust
Then was it there at all
Expand your heart begin to trust
This universal call

IF I COULD HAVE A DREAM, A WISH

If I could have a wish right now
I'd wish the world to take a bow

I'd dream that every eye could see
The answer sits in you and me

If I could have a dream right now
I'd teach each person why and how

There never has to be this pain
If love and balance were sustained

If I could truly have that dream
I'd show that things aren't what they seem

I'd hope that god would give me hands
To help us reach a better land

If I could have a dream right now
I'd ask that Gurus share the Dao

That Monks and Holy men come out
To leave each nation void of doubt

If I could have that dream, that wish
I'd wash their cruel words with a kiss

I'd dream that separation died
While celebrating love inside

If I could make that wish this real
I'd wish each man to also feel

The beauty when the love flows free
I'd wish the world now dream with me

IN ATONEMENT (To the self)

I did not have all the answers
To the questions left inside
Yet the ghosts of old romances
Had no corners left to hide

While my outrage to the outside world
Came bouncing back at me
All the tears of this little girl
Could never set me free

So, I asked the gods inside and out
To hear my loud request
In every whisper and each shout
With thoughts I'd not confessed

To forgive my sins and leave me clean
I'd breached each golden rule
In the darkest places I had been
I'd treat the self so cruel

To forgive my blindness and my spite
With knives I turned on me
I'd plead, for kindness and for sight
With eyes awake to see

I'd plead for less projections
Aimed at spirits who were pure
Then remake me with affections
To help those who've hit the floor

I told gods of many titles
That the peace inside had strayed
That their action now was vital
To withdraw internal blades

I asked gods of all descriptions
To forgive and cleanse my core
Then, to end my hearts afflictions
Making way for open doors

Then, I felt the love beside me
Like an answer to my prayer
As though the gods I thought denied me
Had decided now to care

Then I felt the revelation
Of a point missed from the start
The love craved, and liberation
Had to come from my own heart

So, I told the self I see you
In your childlike lonely place
It's with love I wish to be you
You're the me I'll now embrace

Now, in atonement love is sent
To everything I am within
I now forsake, I now repent
Self-loathing for its sin

INVISIBLE TOUCH

I feel you beside me
Please deter what denies me
Of the light that I see far ahead

I can feel you run through me
Don't give up, please pursue me
Through the part of myself I have fled

I can sense that you know me
So stand up while you show me
A flame shining straight from your heart

I'm aware that you see me
So unlock this and free me
Before this lost spirit departs

I'm aware you observe me
While your love longs to serve me
With the things you're aware I have missed

So start walking towards me
Contradict that which flaws me
Leave the shadows inside of me kissed

I can feel you around me
I've been lost, yet you've found me
Not familiar, yet of this I am sure

That your spirit now holds me
While your warmth now unfolds me
Kindred spirit, we have loved once before

IT'S ALL KUNG-FU
(The beautiful animal forms)

It's still Kung-Fu beyond the fight
Installing freedom, giving sight
Much more than I believed I knew
A way of being within Kung-Fu

Without the science, the form is wrong
While truth to self makes spirit strong
The master sought is inside you
It's activated by Kung-Fu

The ego dies on each new day
While truth is born within 'The Way'
Before you know it you're walking through
Each challenge faced within Kung-Fu

The pecking order makes you less
Look deep inside to find success
Bring love and courage to all you do
Embrace your strength, embrace Kung-Fu

Let go of fear, smash through demise
You're not the prey, become your prize
Turn down the words that make you blue
Become your leader, become Kung-Fu

Each day is met with one more game
Remain objective, hold your frame
Combat each challenge without delay
Remain unscathed within 'The Way'

The Monkey-form can raise the mood
While mocking Jinns as they intrude
Neurotic, ditsy upon first sight
Yet give them cruelty, you'll feel the bite

The Tiger's patience never fails
While tracking every demons trail
He may be brutal without disdain
Yet every strike brakes through the pain

The Eagle flies observing all
It's time to focus when Eagle calls
A heightened vision with wings spread wide
He claws the self-destruct inside

The Panther, fast and so intense
Although short lived, his chi immense
You may need panther in threats unseen
When thoughts get dirty he wipes them clean

The animals, they're all designed
To counter limits within the mind
The obstacles within each day
When met with them can fade away

It's all Kung-Fu, not wrong nor right
To heal thyself means feeling the bite
Fall hard and fast at what life through
Then stand and rise within Kung-Fu

JURISDICTION OF THE WRONG
(Covid-19)

While humankind remain confused
At loss, commands and fear
Kind hearted acts remain abused
Each bully insincere

Unspoken whispers never heard
Pretence bleeds through the mass
Prolonged control in every word
Put there to make us crash

No shouts of hope are screaming out
On every newsflash seen
Why do the leaders feed on doubt
Where has protection been

Let go of simply what we're told
Observe what love can do
Vacate the mindset weak and old
Embrace the strength in you

Hear all they say but step outside
Each word they state as real
A strength in you can swim the tide
Light up the flame concealed

Stand up and see what we can do
Each husband, child or wife
Let go to find the truth in you
For those who've lost their life

LEAVING

He'll leave the days of unseen signs
The times so many crossed his lines

He'll drift away from screaming thoughts
With tightened chains which kept him caught

He'll drift away from binding flesh
And life's cruel rules that made him less

In him it's plain, they see themselves
Reflecting where their sadness dwells

Yet in their blindness they attacked
They blamed him for the truth they lacked

While his intent reached way past pure
This conflict, he can take no more

A building up of others rage
His book now turns it's final page

He knew the mindset, wrote the script
Yet answers found could not predict

Unfounded reasons for their shouts
He spent each moment reaching out

No logic breakdown holds the key
To why he longs to now break free

It's not so much his mental state
Moreover that it's now to late

For one more lesson soaked in blood
From cruelty binding down the good

He'll float away from unheard words
He'll reach the sky and soar with birds

The silence will upstage his thoughts
He'll go back home to all he sought

LET GO OF WHAT IS GONE

I send this out to everyone
No matter who you are

It's time all wrong intent be gone
Where rage has reached too far

I send these words to every soul
Despite the things they do

How can I call my essence whole
Without a hand for you

I send these words to those I've known
In friction and in peace

To friendships gained and those I've blown
May sadness be deceased

Each separate word I weave in lines
Are now sent to you all

Whilst from my heart, I send these signs
With hope you'll hear my call

To those I blamed for bygone grief
To those who sent returns

I love you, way beyond belief
Above responses learned

To those I judged without debate
While breathing words of pride

The time has come, it's not too late
To join as one inside

Yet, equally to those who judged
While fingers wagged and swayed

I now forgive how you begrudged
Through pain inside that stayed

I send these words to those whose hands
Released me from my chains

I love you, try to understand
My lack was blind to gains

These words, I even send to those
Who walked from what they'd see

There is no blame, who could have known
The darkness was not me

Each word is even sent with praise
To strangers in the street

Your smiles helped conquer all those days
Attacked by my defeat

So now I send these words with light
In chapter, verse and song

The strength of love outweighs the fight
Let go of that now gone

LIMITLESS LIMITS (Addiction)

A limit short of solid ground
An overlooked closed door

A balanced voice turned up in sound
A fullness needing more

A signal in the mind shines red
While shouted down by green

Denial grows within her head
The danger goes unseen

The limits tell you when to stop
You overstep the line

The curtains never seem to drop
Its never closing time

What will become of who you are
When waves send you adrift

When breaking limits goes too far
While seeking conscious shifts

The limitless still needs a poise
Whilst chaos has no goal

You lost yourself in all your noise
And sabotaged your soul

LOVE IS ENOUGH

No love need be forsaken
In the essence that we bring
It's in the smallest actions taken
It's the song each robin sings

It's the golden fundamental
It's the reason we exist
Love is truly instrumental
To fix broken hearts we missed

Love is all we've ever needed
To explode internal dams
To uproot the plant once seeded
To make lions from the lambs

Love can be misrepresented
In this world, perceived as weak
Yet, self-love can help repent this
Giving strength for all we seek

Love for self is love for others
Revelations then stand tall
Love for sisters and for brothers
Help us rise from where we fall

Love is truth and love is healing
Find it now with eyes that see
Fill each heartache you're concealing
With the love you're meant to be

MARISA

Marisa, the glow of your beautiful hair
A light in the shadow, were you never aware?

That the tallest of flowers could never compete
Yet you silently fell to your elegant feet

Even your decline exudes a beauty too astounding for eyes
When an encore of angels vibrate in your cries

Beautiful Marisa, their solutions could only fade
In the waves of a truth so much bigger you made

The sadness you carried could not have been wrong
In a world made of tears too deep for your song

Marisa, even love could not explain who you were
Your life was their saviour, your exit a blur

Explanations were lost and words had no place
Yet the answers we sought were received in your grace

Did you ever truly know, feel or see
That the life-force of you is the hope within me?

There really is no end to you because you are not history
I just know you gave me breath albeit in your mystery

Such a beautiful enigma is not described in past tense
When all that she stood for remains so immense

So there can be no goodbye, as you are not gone
You have simply returned to a land you belong

Any sadness now felt must be carried away
In the arms of Marisa still within us today

Marisa, though distant, I know you are here
In my dreams I now see you embracing my fear

As I wake from my sleeping I watch you take flight
Marisa remains a transcendence of light

MISSING – THE ART OF WAR

She'll be missing from moments
They take her for granted
She'll be kissing goodbye to the rules
They once chanted

Missing from eyes left to pry
Without care
Missing, while they question
Just why she's not there

She'll be missing from the board
Of a game they have played
Missing, while foes remain flawed
As she fades

Missing from fields that she walked
With delight
She'll be missing, not caught
As she counters their fight

They'll be missing the prey
That they truly believe
They will soon take away
Viewing her this naive

They'll be missing the structure
Of what she became
They will soon turn to ashes
Outdone by her flame

Yet the light she exudes will be missed
From their view
They'll be missing the structures
In all she can do

They'll be missing the trail
That she moves from their eyes
Left with outcomes that fail
Where they view themselves wise

They'll be missing a point
That was lost in their rules
She went missing by using
Their very own tools

She'll be missing from landscapes
Where the dark vulture flies
She'll go missing, she'll vanish
Right before their own eyes

MORE PRECIOUS THAN COMPLAINT
– FORGIVENESS

I never wore a halo
You could never be a saint
In the name of all that matters
You mean more than my complaint

I could never keep my balance
On the pedestal you made
You could never stay so gallant
On red carpets I had laid

I was never really able
To speak sunshine all the time
While occasionally you made mistakes
They weren't the darkest crimes!

Admittedly when windswept
I lose sense of all composure
Understandably when words are sharp
You morph into exposure

Yet how can it hold significance
Within the greater scheme?
Shall we battle in the nightmare
Or keep fighting for the dream?

The problem is the halo
Sitting heavy on my head
Dictating each angelic word
When truths must now be said

While you have not been knighted
You don't have to be the saint
The value of forgiveness
Is more precious than complaint

MUCH MORE THAN BLOOD OR WATER

In moments past that leave the scar
Of lambs who went to slaughter

I'll tell you this while from afar
We're more than blood OR water

As screaming silence makes its sound
In moments pain is hiding

The bond we share is too profound
Where trivia starts subsiding

No tidal wave in human form
Is bigger than our ocean

A mortal coil cannot be torn
By human man made notion

The friction stands with yesterday
When present starts parading

The angry words we chose to say
In light of NOW start fading

So if today seems cold and bland
Dictating your tomorrow

I'll walk beside you hand in hand
Away from bygone sorrow

Where love is felt and warm winds blow
While lambs are saved from slaughter

Because the you and I we know
Are much more than blood OR water

MY MATRIARCH & FRIEND

Now, with love behind my attitude
To you alone I send
My heartfelt warmth and gratitude
My matriarch and my friend

You weathered every single storm
You never turned your back
To date and from when I was born
You moved my heart from lack

You saw the darker moment
That I wore like second skin
Yet had faith in my atonement
You could see the good within

God knows I made it hard for you
For that, please hear my word
Each kiss and loving thought you blew
Did not once go unheard

The strength you are, you may not know
Yet I can proudly see
That all the gifts I am and show
Is all of you in me

Whilst I could write of flowers
Or of glowing ocean tides
Instead I'll thank you for each hour
You stand there by my side

In moments I have been unwell
You did not show me tears
Instead you pulled me from the hell
Of drowning in my fears

So now I want to give my praise
Though words alone depart
No song nor poem nor sentence says
What you mean to my heart

My greatest friend and Mother
Never change the gift you are
There can truly be no other
In the darkness you're my star

So, with love behind my attitude
To you alone I send
This heartfelt warmth and gratitude
My Matriarch, and my friend

NERVOUS BREAKTHROUGH

Nervous breakthrough
Breaking buildings made of dust
Once sheltered you from skies
Breaking hearts deceived by lust

Leave tears in your eyes
The breaking bridges now collapse
Where once they helped you home
Directions fade upon the maps

There's nowhere left to roam
Breaking patterns on this page
The jigsaw piece won't fit
A sadness takes the seat of rage

The skin you've worn has split
Breaking structures in your mind
While ego breaks the scene
The light breaks through these eyes once blind

Your truth invades your dream
Breaking every story told
Your hands release the script
Your arms begin to loose a hold

Of mirrors always gripped
You're breaking through, not breaking down
You're breaking every chain
You're breaking locks that made the sound

Of never ending pain
You're breaking through the prison walls
Once forced to keep you still
This breaking silence finds the calls

Of freedom, and free will
You're breaking what was never fixed
To fix a broken child
You're breaking through, become enriched
The self is reconciled!

NO ANSWER WAITS OUTSIDE

A lifetime is spent on external solution
Do we ever just pause, stop and wonder
Why we cling to an outside and void resolution
From a ship that is now going under?

No answers are sitting awaiting the self
When sought from a place of such blindness
The key can't be found in a lover nor wealth
The riches come fast in SELF-KINDNESS

The blame can't be cast from a place of transference
Because blame in itself is illusion
There is choice in reaction to every occurrence
A dynamic that is met with confusion

We look at another and feel the burn
Is a lesson left lost in projection?
Do we sit in the darkness or stand up and learn?
Is the 'blame' we believe a deception?

Secondary gains grow in places we hurt
Is it easier to know what is coming?
Is it light you can see or a flashing alert?
You will never find out while you're running

The demons we fear are the ones we create
Yet again each performance is chosen
Why look at THEIR faults before changing YOUR state
We can run with the waves or stand frozen

The seasons will come and the seasons disperse
But we CHOOSE to stand naked in thunder
We can look at the song or start singing each verse
Will your ship set you free or go under?

NOWHERE IS SOMEWHERE

It is far beyond words
To feel this faraway
In a life so absurd
Whilst the night blends with day

There is no concrete ground
Only space upon space
While detached yet so bound
To a path you must face

While your heart seems to cry
Yet the world sees it rise
No concern is applied
To a well-worn disguise

Feeling somewhere astute
Yet you're nowhere at all
There are waves on a route
Made from tears that fall

When their talk seems so right
Yet the heart knows they're wrong
Wide awake yet no sight
Of the land you belong

Yet this nowhere is somewhere
When your eyes see the core
While it seems hard to bear
It's a lesson and more

The outcome exceeds words
Though it seems far away
You'll embrace the absurd
As your night turns to day

If the pain you're releasing
Leaves space for the new
Then the nowhere is somewhere
That somewhere is you

RAISE YOUR HEAD (The Virus)

We know the landscape seems so grey
Where once the sun was bright
Yet you can still direct your day
Bring colour to the night

The future seems to lose its grip
On hope and golden skies
Your dreams are close, don't let them slip
Just raise your head up high

Beyond the forceful governed sound
Beyond the closing doors
There is a beauty so profound
Look up, beyond these walls

Just raise your head to untouched sky
The magic lives and breathes
Where stars still shine, while eagles fly
Just choose to now believe

Raise up your head to see and feel
The nature left unscathed
The beauty there is pure and real
Not silenced, harmed nor slaved

Raise up your head and reconnect
With all you hold inside
Those stars are all that you reflect
Look up, no need to hide

Beyond the media and the fear
Strategic in its form
The hope we crave has long been here
Look up, beyond this storm

Just raise your head to skies above
Release from binding skin
The sky will fill your heart with love
And fill the void within

REACHING DEEP WITHIN (The Virus)

The streets become deserted
While the mass search for a choice
There's no sound where laughter flirted
Just the whisper of one's voice

As we walk through common stomping-ground
We're left to reminisce
On the joy in meeting friends once found
Plus loved ones that we miss

As time goes by so slowly
We don't know when this will end
Through a virus so un-holy
While a government pretends

One thing remains and always will
It's been there all along
Your voice inside when all is still
The sound of your lost song

When the voices that indoctrinate
Shout louder than your heart
Go deep within, it's not too late
To set their sounds apart

When the mass begin to follow
Losing touch with who they are
Not with anger, but with sorrow
Lead them back to guiding stars

The streets may be deserted
Yet, no Kings can take your voice
Let the blind become alerted
To their deeply buried choice

Dictators on their stomping ground
Spout words backed up with sin
You can loose them where your truth is found
When reaching deep within

SAIL AWAY

So now look to the ocean
With wind to your sail

With the footsteps of love
Dented deep on your trail

For your heart is still beating
Inside those that you touched

Now be free from the chains
Of the anchor you clutched

So now drift through the waters
Be out of harm's way

The peaceful waves call you
From the land that you lay

For goodbye is not final
While you're greeting is near

You still walk right beside them
Even if you're not here

As the landscapes you pictured
Showing oceans so blue

They can now become real
Become one within you

While you drift from the mainland
Holding hands with the tide

Let the freedom now hold you
Let the battle subside

Sail away from the carnage
While those close serenade

For your flesh may seem distant
But your love will not fade

So now look to the ocean
With the wind at your sail

Leaving footsteps of love
Dented deep on your trail

SHADOW WATCHERS

I'm watching you, I swear I am
While hearing every door you slam

I'm tracking every step you take
Behind each weak mistake you make

I'm watching whilst you're watching me
Convincing you I'm what you see

I'm watching and I always will
I know your games, I know the drill

I'm watching even with closed eyes
Prepared, aware of your surprise

I watched you thinking I was blind
I watched you fail to ever find

The essence, all which makes me tick
Behind my wall of iron brick

I watched you through a spirits eyes
I saw your lame and cruel disguise

In shadows and in brighter skies
I watched you living out those lies

You watched me, thinking you'd succeed
Your motive came from wrong and greed

You watched me hoping I would break
So unaware of all I'd take

You watched me, every move I made
While hoping all my joy would fade

You watched and watched and hoped I'd tire
So fuelled by gain and self-desire

You watched with patience that's for sure
Yet every game-plan turned out poor

So now I'll watch you from afar
I know your names and who you are

I'll watch you from one step ahead
This target leaves you so misled

I'll watch you while you're self-assured
I'll watch you face the points ignored

You'll watch me, yet you'll always fail
Because you missed me change the trail

SHE WASN'T JUST YOUR NOVELTY

She wasn't just your novelty
A latest fad pursued

She wasn't just an outfit
That you wore when in the mood

She wasn't just a novelty
A recently heard tune

A drug you grew so tired of
When you became immune

She wasn't just a passing phase
Just living for your need

Nor was she just a bandage wrap
To stop your painful bleed

She WAS your playmate as grown ups
She trusted your intention

She lived and breathed your Holy Grail
That you now fail to mention

She never ever doubted you
Whilst others knocked your word

She sings your praises even now
Yet her name goes unheard

You moved away to something new
You grew so very bored

You chased the sounds of hummingbirds
Her song remained ignored

One day you may regret your choice
As you reflect alone

Yet she would always wish you joy
As love is all she's known

One day you may repent your steps
Now she is not enchanted

The lesson lies within the sting
You took her love for granted

TEMPORARY

The only permanent thing we have is the knowledge
That everything is temporary
Silence reminds us gently

That even the sadness, happiness that comes with such
awareness
Just a fleeting moment gone as fast as it arrived
Yet the mind being so contrived

Replaces truth with a false sense of belief in thoughts
of being safe
Inside of many more passing seconds
How the soul beckons

For the adolescent bloom, now unrecognisable as time
Has written scriptures on the blank face of innocence
Though we clutched at time with diligence

The fading child still looks in the mirror and tries to
remember
The point to which he/she became caped in a wise old
souls attire
A silent flame without fire

The internal youngster asking the question is now a fairy
tale
Dancing on the sky line of impermanent memory that
each wise man spectates
Truth now dictates

The solid and safe foundation we seek only strengthens
By truly embracing change
Confronting the strange

To be lost in a memory can only be born from
An expectation that time should stand still for us
Turning life into dust

Yet to walk through memory lane into the present
Is to choose not to stand still for time
The moments we live are the ones we define

THE BEAUTIFUL ELEMENTS

Me is still you, just as you are still me
Whilst you may well be them and they may turn to we

Us turns to those, just as those become them
It began at forever because time has no end

Breath is within us, we all breathe the same
The elements made us before we had names

The blood flows like water, and all of us bleed
The river connects us when we counter the greed

Our feet all touch soil upon the same earth
Mother's soil will absorb us, whilst to us she gave birth

The fire runs through us when we run through the fire
It comes fast in its forms built from flames of desire

While the spirit connects us with all that is one
We go home to this light when we think we are gone

Hence, that I become you just as you become me
Laying down, separation, united, and free

THE C SCARS

The moment may be far away
While times have moved on fast

Where hands reach out for brighter days
So distant from the past

Yet just sometimes I catch the shine
Of mirrors in my sight

Remembering that this flesh is mine
So, marked with every fight

I hear the happy laughing sounds
Behind the tight locked door

While saddened by the scars profound
Left from bad - health before

It's in those seconds feeling lost
I grab each second gained

While gratitude at any cost
Is valued and sustained

The scars don't blend in pretty skin
Or fade like rainy skies

They leave a purple line so thin
The mirror never lies

The scars, a double edging sword
Yet pain brings gratitude

The scars from that which left me floored
In sickness once pursued

The moments may be far away
Like nightmares prove unreal

Yet there is not a single day
I'm free from dread I feel

The scars don't go, they're here, they're mine
Through good times and through strife

Yet each scar gave me strength to shine
The sickness gave me life

THE CHILD THAT SINGS IS THE CHILD IN YOU

The Child sings songs from the
Sheet they don't hear

The child was left as the
Adult drew near

The daisy lit gardens she had
Once seen as home

Became dreams briefly captured
In moments alone

The child, she sings just to feel
Their smile

Left on roads way behind as they
Moved with the miles

The child was stunted
By an internal bleed

While their wounds seem to heal
Her sadness proceeds

She would draw many pictures
Upon their cold walls

They just faded into shadows
Along with her calls

The child is singing from a
Room long ago

Holding blankets for comfort
In a world, she can't grow

The seasons blow past her
Every night every day

Her heart is a child's
Though her blanket it frayed

The child is singing and
Her tune is for you

From the chains of the old
For the love she once knew

The child will cleanse you
In the tears she wept

The child is the part
Of yourself you neglect

THE CRUCIFIXION

His crucifixion
Now conviction
Bible words are bent

The jurisdiction
With restriction
Hides what Jesus meant

I don't do Mass
Yet when I pass
This thing I know for sure

The heart you give
In life, you live
Is what his scripts were for

His sacrificial
Self-dismissal
Seems misunderstood

For those in pain
Out in the rain
Would we donate our blood?

We sing the prayer
Yet are we there
For angels feeling broken

We talk the talk
Yet do we walk
By every word he'd spoken?

While I'm not pure
I know for sure
His selfless incarnation

Was not the sense
Of blind expense
For Christmas celebration

The point is missed
The hands are kissed
Of those who hold the riches

Would we digress
While taking less
To give to those in ditches?

I may seem dark
While seeming stark
I've even toyed with hexing

Yet turn my eye
From those who cry
To me just seems perplexing

He gave his life
We held the knife
The lesson gained in giving

In his advice
Came sacrifice
Give love to those not living

THE CRYING CLOWN

Sometimes he tried and he even felt hope
Loosening the knots that were tying the rope

Sometimes he tumbled back into denial
As he silently screamed through a clowns rosy smile

Then there were moments when he went with the flow
But where others moved forward his mind couldn't go

Then he felt guilty somewhere deep within
Feeling lost in a crisis that was now wearing thin

Those moments soon came feeling left with just self
Spiritual tycoons left him bankrupt of wealth

The Gurus he turned to still came at a price
He tried but he failed to become their advice

What's it about when all said and done
When the clown of the circus could no longer have fun

When the audience applauding the joy that he brought
Could walk from his sadness without word or thought

What are we made of if a human's demise
Can close down our ears whilst blinding our eyes

Expectations of performance dragged the clown to his feet
But his tears were not makeup and inside he felt beat

Sometimes he tried and he even felt hope
As he loosened the knots that were tying the rope

Other times he tumbled back into denial
As he silently screamed through a clown's rosy smile

THE EDGE OF TOMORROW

Tomorrow's edge
Holds close a pledge
Of sleeping eyes awakened

A land now lost
In human frost
Will cease to be forsaken

The atmosphere
Will then be clear
Of doom we sense may beat us

Tomorrow's edge
Holds close a pledge
Today must not defeat us

Those now alone
Becoming stone
Appearing disaffected

Now rest assured
There's many more
Whose hearts have been neglected

The pledge will state
It's not too late
The lonely then will fusion

This synthesis
Will then dismiss
Unwanted dark illusion

Tomorrow's edge
Brings forth this pledge
The shift is way beyond us

Earth's atmosphere
Will cleanse and clear
Polluting waves that wronged us

The open eyes
The old and wise
Perceived as lost and mindless

Will lead the way
From this today
In wisdom and with kindness

Tomorrow's edge
Brings forth this pledge
Right there within that moment

Those wearing crowns
Must put them down
Embracing their atonement

Tomorrow's edge
Holds out this pledge
Its truth will kill confusion

The rogues will guide
Dictators hide
Dismissed from life's illusion

THE GESTAPO ON YOUR PATH

How many are certain that life has been hexed
While silently following orders perplexed

In the land of one's mind where dictators are rife
Making certain that angels are silenced by strife

The Gestapo were planted right there in your thought
As a means of deflecting the freedom you sought

The Gestapo will punish the ones with the flare
Portraying them crazy the moment they dare

They were lodged in the neurons and blocking the gate
Of the magic and laughter giving life to your state

The Gestapo can only stand tall with your word
They can also be finished when your order is heard

The Gestapo were stationed in your mind long ago
Their mission has failed, it is time that they know

The white flag is flying and gripped in your hand
Only YOU give the orders in your unconscious land

THE GOLDEN BOAT WILL CARRY YOU

The golden boat awaits you there
The one within your dream
The one that you were searching for
In every living theme

It now comes forth to carry you
To ease your tired feet
Your angels they will guide you now
Surround you in their fleet

I don't know what was troubling you
A man of so much pride
The struggle threw you to the waves
Now rest in peaceful tides

We had our moments you and I
Communication frayed
I'm grateful that we saw the light
Within the time you stayed

It seems that those who loved you
Truly hung on every word
Yet untrue thoughts that hurt you most
Were silenced and unheard

The golden boat awaits you now
You saw it as you slept
You drifted in the sunlight
As your loved ones sadly wept

The angels they will greet you now
The angry waves will cease
Though loved ones' hearts are hollow
May yours now be filled with peace

THE ICE IS THE WATER
THE WATER IS ICE

The ice is water, the water is ice
Before helping the slaughter, it is time to think twice

We are frozen in climates where the henchmen entice
But we can flow like water, become love born from ice

The ice came from water, we are stagnating ice
Where the freedom of spirit now comes at a price

While mankind's liberation is what lords sacrifice
All the white flowing water turns to cold silent ice

We are pure golden water, forced to freeze into ice
Yet the reasons they're stating still remain imprecise

While the few left unfrozen, they are mocked like small
mice
Just because they have chosen to melt from the ice

We are water so cleansing being frozen like ice
Who knows their next antics, it's a throw of the dice

Yet while pure hearts are beating in this fools paradise
There is hope in defeating the hands that make ice

TRACKED

The source that be is too covert
Designed to crack all those alert

This strategy is so well sewn
That those in charge remain unknown

Yet please believe me when I say
Those in control don't go away

Perceived as bait, they hunt to kill
Direct your thoughts with no self-will

Coincidence will then appear
All made to break the minds they steer

Yet targets keep their lips well sealed
The evidence remains concealed

The verbal threats revealed to few
State 'Who'll believe these words from you'

While solid facts are at ones feet
Each fight obtained still leaves you beat

A label stating 'Paranoid'
Makes you a subject to avoid

Yet in the meantime psychic blades
Slice through the flesh that angels made

They strike at you and break your bones
Then pull you back with loving tones

Don't underestimate effects
Of what dark master's Chi projects

You may be close, you may be far
The masters know just where you are

They're too well hid, they can't be found
Yet henchmen show you they're around

They have a focus in the dark
To utilize your every spark

You're left in silence, what's to say
No shouting stops the games they play

The source that be can leave you hurt
Unless your antics stay covert

Step way ahead of all perceived
With lips well sealed because who'd believe?

Embrace the blows you know are true
Become the flame they want from you

Reflect each bullet, mirror the tools
Of tarnished masters who strive to rule

THE MASTER SITS IN YOU

Some things remain so hard to see
I pray with depth you do

The one you sought to find in me
Sits patiently in you!

The expectations that you hold
Were never viewed as wrong

Yet every story that you told
Are tunes to your OWN song

The torch you held whilst on one knee
You gripped and clutched so tight

I ask the gods that you may see
It's you who holds that light

Each master that you've searched to find
Will always stay concealed

Because that 'Christ' is YOUR own mind
It waits to be revealed

Each word I spoke you viewed profound
Because these words weren't new

They just made way for extra ground
To find what's inside you

Though you have sailed each ocean
Knocked on every temples' door

The Lord you seek, and potions
Can be found within your core

THE PANTHER

The panther will stalk you
This is not about choice

He allures you and walks you
While he speaks through your voice

He cannot be shut down
With suggestion or rules

He's the Panther, renowned
For combatting the fools

The Panther has light
Cutting straight through the meek

He survives day and night
He will find what he seeks

Don't be fooled by the mild
He distracts with his calm

He is primal and wild
Once you're lost in his charms

The panther now beckons
He will not be dismissed

So alive every second
You are prey once you're kissed

Don't dismiss his intention
He is loud, it is clear

No more time for prevention
Now the moon cat be near

THE RAINBOW'S END

I know you, each teardrop you cry
Carries a story hidden deep down within your treasure
box
To which you threw away the key
Yet make no mistake, I could always see

How life became a mass of such confusion
The seasons demolished your breaking illusion

Sunshine, storms, and the tears made from rain
Your heart turned into a hurricane

Even with the coming of summer skies
The haunting thoughts of a gale would follow
Clinging unknowingly to the threads of your sorrow

While doors tried to open to give you shelter
Life had become a helter-skelter

While something inside held on to the preference
Of drowning in a storm, your soul left forlorn
In spite of your loved ones delivering reverence

I knew you
How it cut so deep, in each tear drop leaked
Yet you held the knife in your very own hands

Fingers made of silk reached out to stroke your iron
heart
Yet being so tender, so soft, you remained set apart

The pain within you left in tatters anyone who loved
you,
Anyone who mattered

I watched you
As you allowed yourself to get blown away, day after day
In life's turbulent thunder storms

As you became immune to each life-threatening strike
At one with the pain of life's shattering spikes

THE ROSE-THORN (Jinx)

She looked demure, her form petite
So many got it wrong
Whilst standing small, she wont be beat
So frail, yet, oh so strong

They came in force, and stayed unseen
With finance on their mind
They failed to research where she'd been
Mistaking her for blind

At first she watched through open eyes
At Eastern gifts they gave
A heart so soft, a mind so wise
Her weakness left her brave

The chosen soldier sang his song
While showing her each dance
Manipulation, motives wrong
To draw her into trance

With Eastern promise laced in greed
They watched her flame shine bright
They hoped to see her spirit bleed
Oblivious of her fight

As time passed by, the man they chose
Grew closer to the prey
Ironic how affection grows
For that they meant to slay

The master of this callous clique
So soon became aware
His henchman had become too weak
To leave this rose ensnared

With anger in his every shout
With envy in his heart
He gave out orders void of doubt
To set the two apart

She didn't understand for sure
The reasons for that blow
Their souls were poisoned. far from pure
She couldn't let this go

Confused, with questions in her mind
She gave this sect much thought
Then saw their motives, so unkind
The rose was sold and bought

They distanced he who'd shown her moves
To trap her with his song
That soldier who spoke words to sooth
Was well and truly gone

They'd left her empty of a vice
Which they had built with skill
Yet never once did they think twice
As they pursued their kill

The rose grew stronger than this sect
While blossoming with thorns
They weren't prepared for what affects
A woman deeply scorned

She lived the rule of love and peace
Yet something had to give
The jinx that she would soon release
Would weaken how they lived

She grew and grew, her vigour screamed
She scrutinised their deed
Then, with her tools, the altar gleamed
She planted every seed

She fed the henchmen all they craved
Played into every bid
So soon she'd see each one enslaved
By all the wrong THEY did

Then, one by one they fell from grace
The arrows soared through skies
Though where they came from went untraced
Whilst hidden from their eyes

Her tone so pure, in words she'd sing
Gave way for their neglect
They overlooked a rose-thorn's sting
Their cause came with effect

THE SHADOWS COME FROM LIGHT

She saw your cruel intent right there
Where darker water drips

A loveless spell without a care
Yet witchcraft on your lips

While love of life in all its form
Now underlines the floor

Of wands that conjure up the storm
While closing draughty doors

She saw you ask the gods for wealth
A mantra so naive

To truly gain with love of self
You have to first believe

That all the cloaks and darkened threads
Don't activate the charm

The mystic garments turn to shreds
If others come to harm

She saw you shout intent to gain
In spite of those left bare

She witnessed every fire flame
You charged without a care

Yet in your haste you lost respect
For lessons wizards told

As Father-sky would now reflect
Your roguery three-fold

You undervalued power met
While playing with the night

Yet wiser witches don't forget
That shadows come from light

DON'T LET THE VENOM SCORN YOU

You are beautiful
You're suitable
For life's uncovered stage

With a heart so warm
Please, don't be torn
By those who shout in rage

You are shining
For those pining
To find something deep inside

Now you can show them
And you know them
For the beauty that they hide

Yes, you're older
Yet you're bolder
Inner light dictates the flesh

All you're giving
Helps the living
To rise up from what was less

Yet, some are loathing
In sheep's clothing
All the love you scream and shout

Remain untarnished
By those varnished
As a means to stamp you out

They do not see this
Yet to be this
Will reflect each poisoned song

So watch with sorrow
Their tomorrow
Hands them back each darkened wrong

Yet, you won't hate
Nor underrate
Despite the venom that they speak

Your every sentence
Gives repentance
To the angry and the weak

THE SPIRIT PATH

The path to finding spirit surely means to simply be
Without the flowers in your hair the snobbery and glee

Without the need for those around to recognize your
strength
Surely being spirit is to help the lost at length

The path to being spirit surely doesn't wear a mask
Instead of taking status spirit helps them with the task

Spirit could be wearing combat boots or spikes within
the hair
So long as comfort is received the spirit doesn't care

Surely being spiritual doesn't mean to be aloof
Instead it means to give to those who sleep without a
roof

It surely means to be the action coming from the heart
I'm guessing this would not include to set the poor apart

Surely being spiritual isn't given for the gain
I'm guessing being love does not include to be ordained

I could be wrong but in my time the spirit I recall
Were those not seeking titles as they helped me from my
fall

Surely being spiritual doesn't mean to seek the praise
Instead it means to give some light to those in darker
days

I know that being spiritual can be daily in reprieve
Some days may be agnostic while the next day I believe

Yet this I know and know for sure in every word I say
The one in need could be next door still searching for a
way

To seek the path of spirit doesn't mean to wear a robe
Nor does it mean to find the light by trotting through
the globe

It doesn't call for admiration given by the damned
It surely means to reach out to the ones with dirty hands

The path to being spirit starts with destination self
Be you rolling in the dirt or drowning in your wealth

I'm guessing to be spirit could be lifting those left
floored
If spirit path is what you seek it starts outside your door

THESE DARK ROADS

These dark roads are always winding
Every paving stone I'm finding
Is uprooted by the hands that go unseen

Each direction seems uncertain
With a landscape locked in curtains
Bygone roads won't take me back to where I've been

These dark roads are my wrong turning
Yet a lesson for the learning
But the road I'm on could leave me standing lost

I can't see the destination
Yet my own degeneration
Was the source that put me here at such a cost

I see roadside trees just swaying
Almost like the cold winds saying
We are close to you, yet never to be found

Then the floor erupts beneath my feet
As, once again, I'm feeling beat
Until I find a safer piece of ground

This dark road won't give direction
With no landmarks for detection
As a means of guiding me to safer land

While these lonely hills surround me
Blocking views put there to ground me
I am nowhere in this somewhere that I stand

These dark roads I'm on pursue me
Almost like they always knew me
As I climb I find the bottom at the top

Then, as I see some life before me
Those familiar winds, they call me
While preparing me to walk the walk and drop

These dark roads have hidden meaning
So much more than simply deeming
Me to torture and self-flagellation acts

These dark roads will get much steeper
If my feet don't stamp much deeper
Into every lesson hidden in its cracks

Although this road is cold and binding
If I walk, I'll soon start finding
Every key to set me free from paths of pain

I'll see the terminus for certain
While dark skies will open curtains
Whilst they lift me from this cold familiar lane

THROUGH EMPTINESS

Through emptiness, you'll rise

Who was it you were born to be
Beyond this learned ideal
Strategic lost identities
Illusion posing real

Who are we in this second
If we take away the known
We can find the truth we beckoned
If we exit from the clone

What was the mission planted
Before the thought corrupted light
When eternal freedom granted us
Just life with day and night

Would you know the self, but truly
If corrupted thoughts just crashed
Would your essence 'seem' unruly
As the mirror came to smash

Who are you in your vision
When you cease to be the best
When you walk from the decision
To comply with all the rest

If becoming no one now takes lead
You'll find the truth that hides
You'll grow from every wound that bleeds

Through emptiness, you'll rise

TO JUDGE HER IS TO JUDGE YOURSELF

She stands with scars from what came next
A crowd watch on with eyes perplexed
Yet who are they to write her book
With hands that gave the blows she took

She weathered every hell bent storm
At which point something new was born
Yet even then, the bullets came
From crowds who sought someone to blame

So, who are they to tell her tale?
While putting down her goals, they failed
Then judging actions they've not seen
Condemning paths they've never been

What judgements hold pro-active hearts?
The beating stops where judgement starts
Yet she who loves stays on her knees
To pray for rival's pain to ease

She knows from days of drinking bleach
What self-destructive lessons teach
To hurt the hating comes right back
It kind of makes for self-attack

So now she sees them, no disdain
In words so cruel, they show THEIR pain
Yet nothing shakes the lessons shown
She prays one day they'll find their own

TRUTH

Taste it within each grain that you swallow
The truth becomes solid in thoughts that we follow

To reach is to teach every wave in the mind
That the thoughts we believe are the truths that we find

We awaken when taken to heights not believed
When we turn from the lies and the logic received

When love from above motivates every dream
The tangible essence of life starts to stream

With your power a flower in pure human form
Is the truth they see growing, a rainbow is born

An ideal is real, all we see was once thought
Find your truth in your choice to find all you have
sought

TURN DOWN THE NOISE

The noise gets louder in our ears
A noise soaked up in rules and fears

A noise robotic, low in tone
This noise they make to break our bones

The noise is loud, to some it's heard
The noise that breaks the wings of birds

This noise is toxic, well designed
To numb your soul and break your mind

The noise you hear just keeps on going
To kill your deeper truth and knowing

A noise designed to turn our heads
From golden skies and flower beds

A noise that plays on lack of choice
So loud you'll miss your inner voice

This noise can soon disperse, be gone
If we go back to being one

Their noise, so loud it kills the sound
Of natures beauty all around

It screams its way through natural flows
While killing land where nature grows

The ones of noise are not exempt
From what the natural order meant

For us to heal what this destroys
As one, we MUST turn down their noise

UNSUNG HERO

A human pincushion cannot feel smooth
While accepting the strikes for their pain still not
soothed

With a heart so alive with loving intention
Your actions seemed doomed, without damage
prevention

You were not unaware that the ladder was weak
As you fell to the ground while they reached every peak

Wearing boots sewn together with pure optimism
Seemed a back-handed gift in your every decision

The steps beneath you, they continued to bail
Yet to give to those troubled, not once did you fail

While some gave opinions and protective advice
You gave blood to the dying without once thinking
twice

You preferred the obscure just to give them the fame
While deleting your title to give them a name

You were fading in presence yet increasing your light
Because all their wrong-doings is what made you so
right

WHEN ANGELS TAKE YOU HOME

It's in the end,
Beyond the blend
Of gold and all you own

You'll find they're gone
For right or wrong
When angels take you home

You'll see a light
Beyond the fight
And reason to conform

You'll rise so high
With wings you'll fly
Back home where you were born

Yet, whilst you're here
Please, walk from fear
While facing lessons sent

Turn back and look
Then close the book
No harm to you was meant

When you depart
With just your heart
You'll see the only gold

Was love you shared
In times you cared
For all the hands you'd hold

When stripped of flesh
They will caress
Your error and your flame

You'll blend and flow
Where angels go
With no more guilt nor shame

It's at that end
You'll apprehend
The pain you may have known

You'll finally be
Your truth not seen
When angels take you home

WHO KNEW

Who knew, in truth of the mountains ahead
Or of each shouting nightmare beside you in bed

Who knew in those moments when you burned like a flame
That behind your closed door you were subject to games

Who knew that the heart you left open to all
Was the lifting of others yet the cause of your fall

Who knew that their words were beyond insincere
Yet the lessons they gave you are what brought you here

Who could have known while you drowned with each wave
That by facing the challenge you are left beyond saved

Who could ever have known that the blows you survived
Are the ironic reason you are more than alive

Who could ever have seen that the soul they dismissed
Would one day be the saviour leaving every heart kissed

Who could ever have known that the demons you feared
Were the battles that made you the strength now revered

YOU ARE LOVED

You are very much loved in whatever you do
You are worthy beyond any anger in you

You are valued regardless of moments enraged
You are loved beyond love behind games you have staged

You truly are loved when you loathe your whole self
You are loved when with nothing, and loved in your
wealth

You are loved when connected, and you're loved when
you're blind
You are loved when you're hurting and becoming unkind

You are loved in your armour, and so loved standing bare
Very loved in your presence, deeply loved when not there

Loving love still surrounds you while you turn from your
heart
The love grows much stronger when you choose to go
dark

You are loved while expressing all this rage at the mass
You are loved as you carry any pain from your past

You are loved within silence, and so loved when in strife
Now acknowledge your value, be the love of your life

YOU ARE

YOU are the master you wished for and sought
YOU are the eraser wiping out what was taught

YOU are the one now activating the dream
YOU are also the one who is more than you seem

YOU are not just a body bound together with flesh
YOU are not just a concept depicted as less

YOU are not obligated to a title you've signed

You ARE free to question everything that you know
You ARE free to change paths just to see where they go

You ARE free to collapse the illusion of fear
You WILL see in that moment there is no nightmare here

You can NOW make a choice without thoughts from the
left
You can NOW embrace loss without feeling bereft

You can NOW become frequency minus a view
You can NOW become no one if it means finding you

FREE to know all the answers are sitting inside
FREE to know that the landscape is open and wide

FREE to know your ability outweighs your belief
The gateway to YOU is the door to relief

YOU

Although it seems the day looks stark
Whilst stars, they fade behind the dark
In turn the joy has lost its song
You question now where you belong

When loved ones seem so lost in time
While tunes of joy have left their rhyme
To even know these things exist
Could indicate a point you missed

The pleasant things you ponder on
Suggests a golden song not gone
For all this beauty that you see
Comes from perception that you be

The golden glow is in all things
While born from joy the viewer brings
The night makes way for stars to shine
Within each loss, the strength you find

In having nothing, all is found
Internal richness so profound
The walk of pain leads to the cure
Embracing less, you learn much more

So, if today seems flat and stark
Look to the stars before the dark
The joy is there, it needs your song
Become what's right, in times so wrong

Georgia Brown is a prolific writer of poetry and has a vlog post on social media where she reads aloud her work. I feel however when reading her work one gets a sense of the emotions of Georgia at the time of writing. Her poetry runs the gamut of her emotions such as love, compassion, sadness, despair & anguish. I do find her rhythmical phrasing of her chosen words remarkable.

Having known Georgia for many years she very quickly became my go to friend and loyal confidant. Her knowledge of allsorts of stuff constantly amazes me. I originally was told by many people to keep away from Georgia due to her nefarious past. I urge you to ignore all that and you will find within her poetry the true glorious character of a very, very creative and special human being.

ViC Gilmore – Musician & Friend

CONTACT

❖

E: info@georgiaism.co.uk
W: georgiaism.co.uk
F: facebook.com/georgiaism
Y: youtube.com/georgiaism
I: instagram.com/georgiaismbrown
T: twitter.com/georgiaism
Tk: tiktok.com/@georgiaism